SMART ABOUT
Art

Edgar Degas
Paintings that Dance

Written and illustrated
by
Maryann Cocca-Leffler

Grosset & Dunlap · New York

This book is dedicated to my editor, Jane O'Connor.
Thank you for believing in me.—Maryann

Acknowledgements:
Special thanks to Kate Bussard and Alexis Goodin
of the Clark Art Institute, Williamstown, Massachusetts,
for making the Degas collection available to me,
and to Judy Romein, reference librarian
of the Amherst Public Library, Amherst, New Hampshire.

Cover: Edgar Degas, *The Dancers*, pastel on paper, about 1899. Toledo Museum of Art, Toledo, Ohio; Purchased with funds from the Libbey Endowment, Gift of Edward Drummond Libbey.

Library of Congress Cataloging-in-Publication Data
Cocca-Leffler, Maryann, 1958–
    Edgar Degas : paintings that dance / written and illustrated by Maryann Cocca-Leffler.
    p. cm.
    Written as a report by a fictitious student.
    1. Degas, Edgar, 1834–1917—Juvenile literature. 2. Painters—France—Biography—Juvenile literature.
[1. Degas, Edgar, 1834–1917. 2. Artists.] I. Title.
    ND553.D3 C63 2001
    709'.2—dc21
    [B]
ISBN 0-448-42611-0 (GB)   B C D E F G H I J   2001023149
ISBN 0-448-42520-3 (pbk)   J

From the desk of
Ms. Brandt

Dear Class,

Our unit on famous artists is almost over. I hope that you enjoyed it as much as I did.

I am excited to read your reports. Here are some questions that you may want to think about:

- Why did you pick your artist?

- If you could ask your artist 3 questions, what would they be?

- Did you learn anything that really surprised you?

Good luck and have fun!

Ms. Brandt

Edgar Degas
My Artist

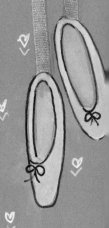

Every night before I go to sleep, I look at the poster over my bed. It is a painting by Edgar Degas called *The Dance Class.*

In the painting, some dancers are practicing, while others are waiting. Their mothers are in the background watching. This painting reminds me of my ballet class.

I love this poster. That is why I picked Edgar Degas for my report. But now I know that he painted many other things besides ballet dancers.

KRISTIN

MY CAT

TWINK TOES

The Dance Class, by Edgar Degas. 1876. The Metropolitan Museum of Art. Bequest of Mrs. Harry Payne Bingham, 1986. (1987.47.1) Photograph © 1987 The Metropolitan Museum of Art

See the girl biting her nails? She looks nervous. I know how she feels. My next recital is coming up soon!

ME →

Young Edgar

Edgar Degas was born in Paris, France, on July 19, 1834. Edgar had two brothers and two sisters. He was the oldest.

Edgar's father | Edgar's mother | Edgar | Achille | Thérèse | Marguerite | René

His family was rich. Their house was big and fancy and filled with beautiful paintings. His father took him to many museums. Edgar liked to spend hours looking at famous paintings.

When Edgar was twelve years old, he was sent away to a school for boys. It was very strict. He had to wear a uniform. He had to march to his classes. That doesn't sound very fun to me.

thought you said Edgar's name like this: "Day Gas." but I was wrong. You say it like this: "Day Gah."

Detail of signature from *Jockey on a Rearing Horse*, by Edgar Degas. Sterling and Francine Clark Art Institute, Williamstown, Massachusetts

That's how he signed his artwork.

He went to this school for seven years. Edgar took art classes. I was surprised to learn that his marks in drawing class were not very good!

Still, Edgar wanted to be a painter. The trouble was, his father did not like the idea at all!

He made Edgar go to law school. But Edgar quit law school.

LAWYER!

PAINTER!

Edgar followed his dream and left home to become a painter. After a while, his father stopped trying to make Edgar be a lawyer. He sent him to the School of Fine Arts in Paris. I'm glad Edgar's father changed his mind.

Edgar's Early Paintings

Edgar spent a lot of time at the Louvre Museum in Paris. He also traveled to many museums in Italy. Edgar thought he could become a better artist by copying famous paintings. He tried to make his artwork look like these paintings.

This painting is by the famous artist Rembrandt. He was one of Edgar's favorite painters. Rembrandt was twenty-seven years old when he painted this picture of himself.

Portrait of the Artist in a toque and a gold chain, by Rembrandt van Rijn.
Musée du Louvre. Réunion des Musées Nationaux/Art Resource, NY

Here is my self-portrait. I did this by looking in the mirror

Edgar painted this picture of himself when he was twenty-three. This is called a "self-portrait." He has on a smock and a red scarf. Doesn't he look like an artist?

K.C.

Edgar
Painter of Everyday Life

One day, Edgar met a famous painter. He looked at Edgar's artwork. He told him to stop copying paintings in the museum. He told him to draw all the time, no matter where he was.

CAFÉ

L'Absinthe, by Edgar Degas. 1875–76. Photo: Herve Lewandowski. Réunion des Musées Nationaux/Art Resource, NY

Millinery Shop, by Edgar Degas. 1884–90. Mr. and Mrs. Lewis Larned Coburn ...orial Collection, 1933.428. Photograph courtesy of The Art Institute of Chicago.

BALLET

L'Etoile, Dancer on the Stage, by Edgar Degas. Musee d'Orsay.
Photo credit: Erich Lessing/Art Resource, NY

HAT
SHOP

That's just what Edgar did! He drew and drew. He took his sketchbook everywhere. He went to the opera and to the ballet. He went to the local laundry, hat shops, and cafés.

OLD PAINTING

Soon, Edgar's pictures began to change. He stopped painting fancy people just standing around doing nothing.

Achille De Gas in the Uniform of a Cadet, Edgar Degas, Chester Dale Collection. Photograph © 2000 Board of Trustees, National Gallery of Art, Washington D.C.

This was how he used to paint.

Here is a painting of Edgar's brother, Achille. Achille had to stay still for hours so that Edgar could sketch and paint him. (That's amazing! My brother can't sit still for two seconds!)

NEW PAINTING

Now Edgar began to draw people doing everyday things, like combing their hair, bathing, ironing, or dancing.

This was his new way of painting.

Sometimes Edgar sketched the same model in different positions. Then he would put them together in one painting. In this painting, the girl combing her hair is the same girl shown three times.

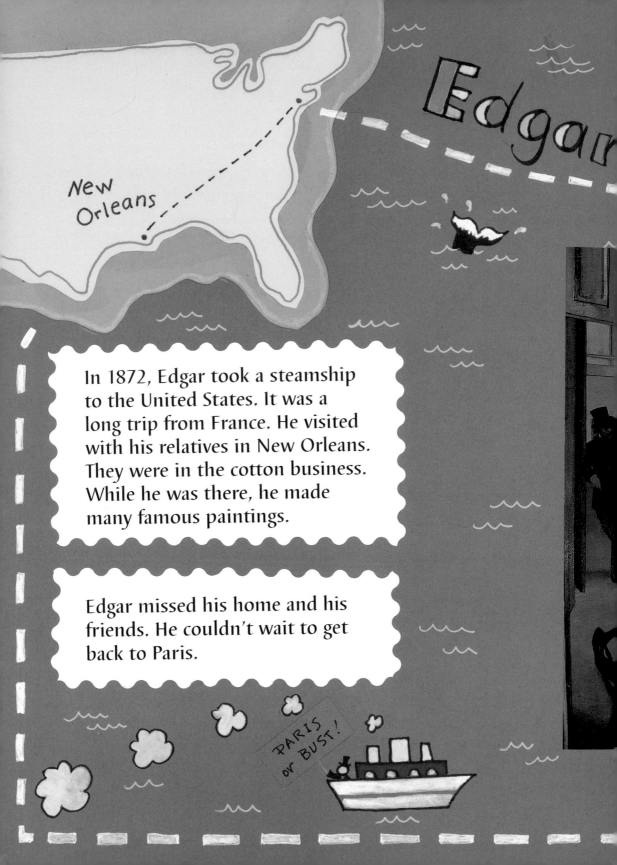

New Orleans

Edgar

In 1872, Edgar took a steamship to the United States. It was a long trip from France. He visited with his relatives in New Orleans. They were in the cotton business. While he was there, he made many famous paintings.

Edgar missed his home and his friends. He couldn't wait to get back to Paris.

PARIS or BUST!

travels to **U.S.A.**

Paris

The Cotton Exchange, New Orleans, 1873, by Edgar Degas (1834–1917) Musee des Beaux-Arts, Pau, France/Bridgeman Art Library

Edgar's two brothers are in the painting. René is reading the paper. Achille is leaning on the windowsill.

Edgar: an Indoor Artist

Many of Edgar's friends were also painters. Their names were Claude Monet, Paul Cézanne, Mary Cassatt, and Vincent van Gogh. His friends liked to paint outside in the sunlight. They painted fields and mountains and flowers.

Edgar, Come out!

Monet →

Mont Sainte-Victoire and the Viaduct of the Arc River Valley, by Paul Cezanne. Credit: The Metropolitan Museum of Art, H.O. Havemeyer Collection, Bequest of Mrs. H.O. Havemeyer, 1929. (29.100.64) Photograph © 1979 The Metropolitan Museum of Art

Cézanne

Edgar Come Out!

Women at the Garden at Ville d'Avray, by Claude Monet (1840–1926). Musée d'Orsay. Photo: Herve Lewandowski. Réunion des Musées Nationaux/Art Resource, NY

Edgar Degas was different. He liked to paint indoors in his studio. He would gather all the sketches that he had done around town. Then he would paint the picture using oil paints.

Woman Ironing, by Edgar Degas, Collection of Mr. and Mrs. Paul Mellon, Photograph © 2000 Board of Trustees, National Gallery of Art, Washington, D.C.

Edgar bought lots of paintings from his friends. It was like he had his very own museum. But not many people got to see these paintings. Edgar liked to be by himself in his crowded studio.

Illustration from *One Hundred of Women*, by Nishikawa Suker © Copyright The British Museu

Do you believe he even had a full-sized stuffed horse in his studio? Well, he did!

Edgar also had lots of Japanese prints. He had one over *his* bed, just like I have an Edgar Degas poster over my bed! He liked the way that Japanese artists showed the beauty and pleasure of everyday life.

bing the Hair ('La Coiffure'), by Edgar Degas. c.1896 © National Gallery, London

This is
a Japanese
print.

↑ This is Edgar's
painting.

They are different in some ways.
They are the same in other ways.

Edgar and Photograph

A Woman Seated Beside a Vase of Flowers, by Edgar Degas. 1865. The Metropolitan Museum of Art, H.O. Havemeyer Collection, Bequest of Mrs. H.O. Havemeyer, 1929 (29.100.128). Photograph © 1998 The Metropolitan Museum of Art

In one book I read, it said that Edgar Degas's paintings are a little like photographs. They are "snapshots of life." I think I understand what that means. Just like in photographs, sometimes part of the body is cut off.

My Mom.

Here is a photo I took. I was trying to make it look like Edgar's painting.

I found out that Edgar sometimes took photographs to help him with his paintings. Here is a photograph he took. It is of a dancer.

Photo of a dancer, by Edgar Degas.
Cliché Bibliotheque Nationale de France, Paris.

The Ballet

Dancers, Pink and Green, by Edgar Degas. The Metropolitan Museum of Art, H.O. Havemeyer Collection, Bequest of Mrs. H.O. Havemeyer, 1929 (29.100.42). Photograph © 1986 The Metropolitan Museum of Art

ME

Edgar liked to show movement in his paintings.
I guess that is why he loved to paint ballet dancers.
He studied the dancers backstage before the
big performance.

We do all the same things...tie our ballet shoes, stretch, practice at the barre, and rehearse.

The Dancing Lesson, by Edgar Degas, c.1880. Sterling and Francine Clark Art Institute, Williamstown, Massachusetts

He learned all the ballet steps so he could paint them. I wonder if he practiced with the dancers? If he came to my class, I could teach him all the positions.

The "Little Dancer"

Sometimes he invited dancers to pose for him in his studio. They would do "still poses." That means they had to hold still for a long time while he sketched them.

Marie

One of these dancers was his fourteen-year-old neighbor. Her name was Marie van Goethem. Marie was the model for my favorite piece of artwork. It is called *Little Dancer, Fourteen Years Old.*

Edgar did many sketches of Marie.

Detail of *Three Studies of a Dancer in Fourth Position*

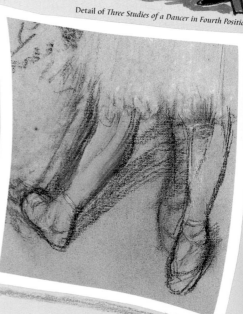

Detail of *Three Studies of a Dancer in Fourth Position*

s is me in the "Little Dancer" pose.

charcoal gets messy!

Holding is position is hard work!

A charcoal stick

Edgar used charcoal for his sketches.

Studies of a Dancer in Fourth Position

Three Studies of a Dancer in Fourth Position, Edgar Degas, c.1879/80, Bequest of Adele R. Levy, 1962.703. Photograph courtesy of The Art Institute of Chicago.

Surprise!

"Little Dancer" is not a painting! It's a Sculpture!

The Little Dancer of Fourtee[n] Years, by Edgar Degas. Ste[rling] and Francine Clark Art Ins[titute] Williamstown, Massachus[etts]

From his many sketches, Edgar made many practice sculptures.

Edgar worked on the sculpture for four years. The sculptures were made out of wax.

Many years later, lots of bronze copies were made of the Marie sculpture. They are in museums all over the world. I got to see one at a museum. It was awesome!

This is one of the many bronze copies. Each museum dresses it in a different tutu.

Little Dancer' Facts

The wax dancer was painted and then dressed in real clothes.

When people first saw the sculpture, they thought that it was ugly. I think it is beautiful.

Everything was covered with wax, except for the tutu and hair ribbon.

...e story is that a ...ollmaker made the tiny ...allet slippers, the tutu, and ...ne wig made of real hair.

this is the back → view

The *Little Dancer* is about 39" tall. I am 52" tall. I was surprised. I thought she was going to be bigger than me.

An X-ray was taken. Inside, holding up the sculpture, was a "skeleton" made of wire and broken wooden paintbrushes.

Little Dancer Aged Fourteen, by Edgar Degas. 1881. Joslyn Art Museum, Omaha, Nebraska. Gift of M. Knoedler & Co., Inc., New York

Edgar also liked to go to the racetrack. He would sketch horses and their riders. Then guess what he did. Edgar brought his sketches home and painted in his studio.

Race horses in front of the stands, by Edgar Degas, 1866-1868. Photo: Herve Lewandowski. Musee d'Orsay. Credit: Reunion des Musees Nationaux/Art Resource, NY

Just like his ballet paintings, he showed the horses and riders before the race…like dancers waiting backstage.

paintings

This is one of Edgar's sketches.

Detail of *Jockey on a Rearing Horse*, by Edgar Degas, Sterling and Francine Clark Art Institute, Williamstown, Massachusetts

Before the Race, by Edgar Degas, c.1882, Sterling and Francine Clark Art Institute, Williamstown, Massachusetts

Edgar's Last Years

As Edgar grew older, he began to lose his eyesight. Edgar did more sculptures in wax. But most of the time, he drew with pastels. He used big strokes. I love the bright colors.

Entrance of the Masked Dancers, by Edgar Degas. 1884. Sterling and Francine Clark Art Institute, Williamstown, Massachusetts

Pastels are FUN!

My Pastel →

Edgar's Pastel

f Entrance of the Masked
by Edgar Degas. 1884.
and Francine Clark Art
, Williamstown, Massachusetts

This is what his strokes look like up close.

This is a photograph of Edgar taken when he was older. He looks very serious—maybe he's thinking about all of the paintings he's done!

Edgar Degas died on Sept. 27, 1917. He was 83 years old.

Detail of portrait photograph of Edgar Degas (1834–1917) and Zoe (b/w photo) Private Collection/Roger-Viollet, Paris/Bridgeman Art Library

Edgar worked as an artist all his life. He never married or had children. If I met my artist, what would I ask him? I don't think I would want to meet Edgar Degas! I found out that he was grouchy all the time. I'd rather just look at his beautiful artwork. (But I'm really glad he didn't become a lawyer!)

Kristin, you did a wonderful report. My favorite Degas is "The Little Dancer," too! I love sculpture, because it is 3-D. You can walk around one piece and look at it from so many sides. It will look completely different depending on where you are standing!

Ms. Brandt